A Guaranteed Smile

JOHN GRANT

ISBN 978-1-68570-254-0 (paperback)
ISBN 978-1-68570-255-7 (digital)

Christian Faith Publishing
832 Park Avenue
Meadville, PA 16335
www.christianfaithpublishing.com

Printed in the United States of America

Smiles

Smiles are simple, and they're easy to do
and each smile you see is a smile that is brand-new.
Up to the ears and away from the chin
without any effort a smile begins:
They speak every
language, and they can't be denied
because our smiles are special and too hard to hide.
With a softness that is contagious and the strength of steel,
simple little smiles change how we feel.
Every smile is unique: your smile is too,
in fact, my favorite smile is the smile God gave to you!

Beautiful Goodbye

The greatest gift you could give to another is your time
and I wanted to thank you for your time.
I hope the time you spent with me
was worth a memory
because all the places we would go and all
the things that we would do
created a special place in my heart just for you.
I can't remember the reasons, so there's no one to blame.
I just know the love we shared is no longer the same.
We relished in the joy of love, and alone we will endure its pain.
We were lovers yesterday maybe friends in the distant tomorrow.
I will remember all the good times and forget about all the sorrow.
Thank you for your time.

Little Ray of Light

Little ray of light, I feel your warmth within my soul,
you bring forth the beauty of the world and the best within us all
Little ray of light, you fall from heaven through the sky
you brighten even my darkest days and
make that twinkle in my eye.
You smile a new day with all of your light,
and you leave us your warmth when you leave for the night.
Now I know until life ends, your light will never fade
because little ray of light, you are the
greatest gift God has ever made.

The Heights of Love

The heights of love are endless we both know it's true,
only I have never known a love like the love I share with you;
Take my hand, don't be afraid, we will soar
to heights few will ever know.
We will relish in love's joy and endure its pain as one,
but remember, don't let go because the best is yet to come.

Like the Wind

It comes at you from all directions, from a gentle
breeze to a powerful gust, it can lift you, it can
move you, it can knock you down. Unpredictable
and mysterious, it will let you fall with no
resistance while an airplane glides on its surface. It's
always at my back, as it moves me along, it
swirls beneath my feet, lifting me as I go. Moving
so fast, it makes me spin my feet above my
head and then under me again then it starts this
dance all over again. In many ways, you are like
the wind, gentle and powerful. You always have my
back, sweeping me off my feet and when I
see you I begin to spin I want to dance with you
all over again in many ways you are just like
the wind I love the way you move me

The Face

The face the front of the mask of the mind
A clever disguise we all hide behind;
Two lips, a nose, and a pair of eyes
Each of the same just a different disguise. Who
lies behind your mask when your face
lies for you a tale by one or a fable by two or
is the lie who you aren't but who you
portray yourself to be a disguise so perfect
we see who you want us to see.
Your mask has a smile yet your face has a frown
On the outside you're happy, on the inside you're down,
or could it be it's the other way around?
Your face can lie to me, and your mask can say it's true.
Sometimes, we have one face, sometimes, we have two.
Look into the mirror, do you see a face or a facade?
You can hide behind your mask when you hide the truth from me.
Only you don't have to live a lie when the truth will set you free.

Styles

Styles come and styles go what's in style
you have to know someone who knows someone
to know what is a style. How long do they last? Some last a while
while others fade fast. Some styles return, yet again,
They will fade replaced by another somebody made.
Look at that watch, check out those shoes.
That's a nice car, Cristal's the cool booze
Do any of those things make life worthwhile?
They do nothing for me you
see that's just not my style.

Graced

How this world came to be
We may never know;
We were graced with this life
The mountains, the streams,
The infinite beauty of the world
That inspires our dreams;
Inside this globe of magnificent wonder
Are billions of minds. Each mind has its own thunder
Each mind is a face dancing in time
I was graced with the miracle, your face found mine.

A Diamond

A diamond is just a simple stone; A true craftsman and his
imagination forged a jewel beyond our imagination;
It will hypnotize, mesmerize, holds you captive the moment it
meets your eyes; It's known around the world as the symbol for
love,
Elegance, and grace; So it's no wonder when I gaze into a
diamond; I see your face

Crystal Ball

If I had a crystal ball, I wonder
Would it show me all? Like what my life might someday be,
I really wonder what I might see.
Could it show me why people like myself,
place our dreams upon a shelf. We think that
life is make-believe, but it's our own hearts that we deceive.
If I had a crystal ball, would it show me how
to live my life? Could it tell me
how to live life right?
Or would it tell me that my life is up to me,
and all the answers are inside of
me. So if I had a crystal ball, I hope I don't
have to ask it why I didn't change
anything at all

Time

As I fell from your grace, I landed soft upon a cloud.
I hoped that you could hear my voice as I
called your name out loud because I believe the
time we shared was nothing short of love and
again, I believe, it could be with just a gentle little
shove when I reach out to hold your hand it
vanishes in time and I try to kiss your lips through
the bars of our minds. But if you look into your
heart you will find, there is a key that will free me
from the chains that keep you away from me.

Moments

The moments that make up a lifetime are etched
within our soul. They are the lessons we learn
and the achievements we earn, the essence of who
we are. There are moments of love, moments
of joy, and moments our hearts break in two. There
are moments we will never forget, and
moments we will always regret, and we move on to
something new. Not a moment too soon or a
moment too late, the moment we decided to try.
Moments of change, moments we don't, those
moments are up to you. Fate is the moment you
find the one to share the rest of life's moments
with you.

Beautiful

Words that describe your beauty elude me; You can see it
Inside of my smile.
The way it lights up as you walk by,
And lingers after you've gone; I notice the colors are brighter;
The sounds clearer
My heart quickens with your charm
And your grace
Everything about you makes my heart race;
When it comes to describing beauty
like yours, words
Will always fall short; It's beauty you feel, it sets you free. It's
beauty anyone that looks at you can see.

About the Author

My name is John Grant I am one of eight children, two biological siblings and five step siblings. I have three children of my own, My daughter Blaire, my son Jon-Michael and my youngest son David. they make me smile every day. I was born November 19, 1965 I am a Colorado Native and love living here. I enjoy the mountains year round and find summers in Colorado the best. I guarantee you will smile when you read my book or you can have your frown back.